Dinosaurs
Dougal Dixon

KINGFISHER

KINGFISHER

First published 2010 by Kingfisher
an imprint of Macmillan Children's Books
a division of Macmillan Publishers Limited
20 New Wharf Road, London N1 9RR
Basingstoke and Oxford
Associated companies throughout the world
www.panmacmillan.com

Illustrations by: Peter Bull Art Studio
Additional illustrations by: Steve and Sam Weston;
Russell Gooday and Jon Hughes/Pixel Shack

ISBN 978-0-7534-1899-4

Copyright © Macmillan Children's Books 2010

1 3 5 7 9 8 6 4 2

1TR/0310/UNT/WKT/157MA/C

A CIP catalogue record for this book is available from
the British Library.

Printed in China

Picture credits

**The Publisher would like to thank the following
for permission to reproduce their material.
(t = top, b = bottom, c = centre, l = left, r = right):**
Pages 4br Corbis/Louie Psihoyos; 5cl Shutterstock/Paolo
Toscani; 5bl Shutterstock/JuNe74; 8cl Shutterstock/Wesley
Pohl; 9tl Shutterstock/Anton Foltin; 9bl taburinsdino; 11br
Shutterstock/wupeng; 12cl Corbis/DK Limited; 12b Natural
History Museum, London; 13cl Natural History Museum,
London; 13ctr Shutterstock/Palis Michalis; 13cbr Natural
History Museum, London; 13br Corbis/Sandy Felsenthal;
15tr Corbis/ Louie Psihoyos; 16bl Mervyn Rees/Alamy;
17c Natural History Museum, London; 19br Getty
Images/National Geographic; 21t Getty Images/Dorling
Kindersley; 23tr Nature Picture Library/Jose Luis Gomez
de Francisco; 24 Natural History Museum, London;
25tl Corbis/Louie Psihoyos; 25tr Corbis/Louie Psihoyos;
25cl Natural History Museum, London; 29t Corbis/HBSS;
29bl Corbis/Bernardo Gonzales Riga; 29br Corbis/Louie
Psihoyos; 30cr Shutterstock/Juriah Mosin; 30br
Shutterstock/Anton Foltin; 31 Shutterstock/slowfish

Contents

Choose your own journey

On some of the pages in this book, you will find coloured buttons with symbols on them. There are four different coloured buttons, and each belongs to a journey you can follow through the book. Choose a journey, and follow it through the book, and you'll find you make some interesting discoveries of your own.

For example, on page 7 you'll find a red button next to a pack of hunting dinosaurs, like this:

Page 22

Food and feeding

There is a page number in the button. Turn to that page (page 22) to find something else about food and feeding. Follow all the steps through the book, and at the end of your journey you'll find out how the steps are linked, and discover even more information about this topic.

Science

Dinosaur lives

Nature

The other journeys in this book are science, dinosaur lives and nature. Follow a journey and see what you can discover!

What were dinosaurs?

The dinosaurs were a group of reptiles that lived between 230 and 65 million years ago. They were the most important land animals during the Triassic, Jurassic and Cretaceous periods of Earth's history.

Dinosaurs came in a variety of shapes and sizes. There were pack-hunting animals, like these Coelophysis, giant hunters and all sorts of plant-eaters.

Dinosaurs laid eggs, as reptiles do today. Many even made complicated nests and looked after their young, like birds.

Triceratops lived
at the end of the
Cretaceous
period.

The Cretaceous period (120 million years ago to 65 mya) saw the last of the dinosaurs. All kinds of armoured and horned dinosaurs appeared.

Jurassic times (180 mya to 120 mya) were the dinosaurs' heyday. Large meat-eaters evolved, and the long-necked plant-eaters became the biggest land animals ever.

Diplodocus was a
Jurassic plant-eater.

Many dinosaurs had scaly skin.

These leathery, dinosaur-like scales belong to a modern crocodile.

By the end of the **Triassic period** (208 mya) there were all kinds of dinosaur groups, including the first big plant-eaters.

Plateosaurus
was an early
plant-eater.

Today's reptiles, like this gecko, have **legs** that stick out to the side. Dinosaurs held their legs beneath their heavy bodies.

The earliest dinosaurs appeared in the late Triassic period around 230 mya. They were swift two-footed hunters.

Eoraptor was
one of the first
dinosaurs.

Page 15

What is this?

1 Diplodocus, a big plant-eater

2 Allosaurus uses its claws to kill and to tear meat.

3 Allosaurus, the biggest Jurassic meat-eater

Meat-eaters

Today, meat-eating animals eat plant-eating animals. It was exactly the same in dinosaur times. In the Jurassic period, about 150 million years ago, fierce meat-eating dinosaurs were hunting all over the world.

Page 22

6

4

A pack of hungry Ceratosaurus settles down to eat its kill – a baby Diplodocus. But then a giant Allosaurus leaps in to chase them away and steal the meal. While the fight rages, a swift little Ornitholestes nips in and snatches away a tasty piece of meat.

5

? This is the big killing claw of an Allosaurus.

Fierce killers

If you look at a dinosaur skeleton, you can usually tell straight away if it was a meat-eater. Look for long jaws with sharp teeth, and clawed hands. You'll see strong back legs for running and a small body balanced by a heavy tail.

Back is held level, so that the teeth and claws are well forward.

Hands and claws are held inwards for seizing.

The meat-eating dinosaurs are called theropods.

The teeth at the side of Albertosaurus jaws (above top) were flat blades, like steak knives, for cutting meat. Those at the front (above) were thicker, for holding on to struggling prey.

Giganotosaurus was one of the largest of all meat-eaters. Over 12 metres long, it could attack and kill the biggest of the plant-eating dinosaurs in Late Cretaceous South America.

Allosaurus

Meat-eaters had three-clawed toes.

stiff, heavy tail for balance

Strong hind legs carried the whole of the dinosaur's weight.

Allosaurus was the biggest of the Jurassic meat-eaters. It stalked the plains of North America, attacking giant plant-eaters, or stealing the prey killed by smaller hunters.

Meat-eater skulls had flexible jaws that could open wide and swallow huge chunks of meat. Some were heavy and worked like hammers, bringing the upper teeth crashing down with killing force.

Ceratosaurus skull

Allosaurus used both its teeth and its claws for killing.

Jurassic giants

The heaviest, longest and tallest animals ever to have lived on land were the sauropods. These plant-eating giants spent most of their days eating, munching through enormous amounts of food. They had long necks and tiny heads.

Page 23

Page 27

1 Diplodocus, a very long sauropod

2 Diplodocus eating leaves with its rake-like teeth

3 monkey-puzzle tree, a typical Jurassic tree

? This is a close-up of a young cycad leaf, a favourite food for sauropods.

3

The plains of Jurassic North America are dry places. Trees grow only along river banks and around lakes. The ground is covered by low-growing ferns and cycads. Big sauropods roam the landscape, eating this vegetation. Pairs of tall Brachiosaurus browse the high branches, like giraffes. Other sauropods feed on the middle branches or close to the ground.

6

Page 22

4

5

What is this?

4 Camarasaurus, the most common Jurassic sauropod

5 Brachiosaurus, one of the tallest sauropods

6 Brachiosaurus eating high branches

Plant-eating machines

The long-necked sauropods, the biggest land animals that ever lived, were all plant-eaters and ate huge amounts of food. We can tell a lot about these dinosaurs from fossils of their long necks, stomach insides and teeth.

Some sauropods had spines down their backs and clubs on their tails.••••

A scientist builds a model of a sauropod skeleton.

A Diplodocus skeleton shows its tail held off the ground and its neck held low. When it was alive, both were pulled up by strong tendons along the backbone.

Diplodocus was the longest-known sauropod.

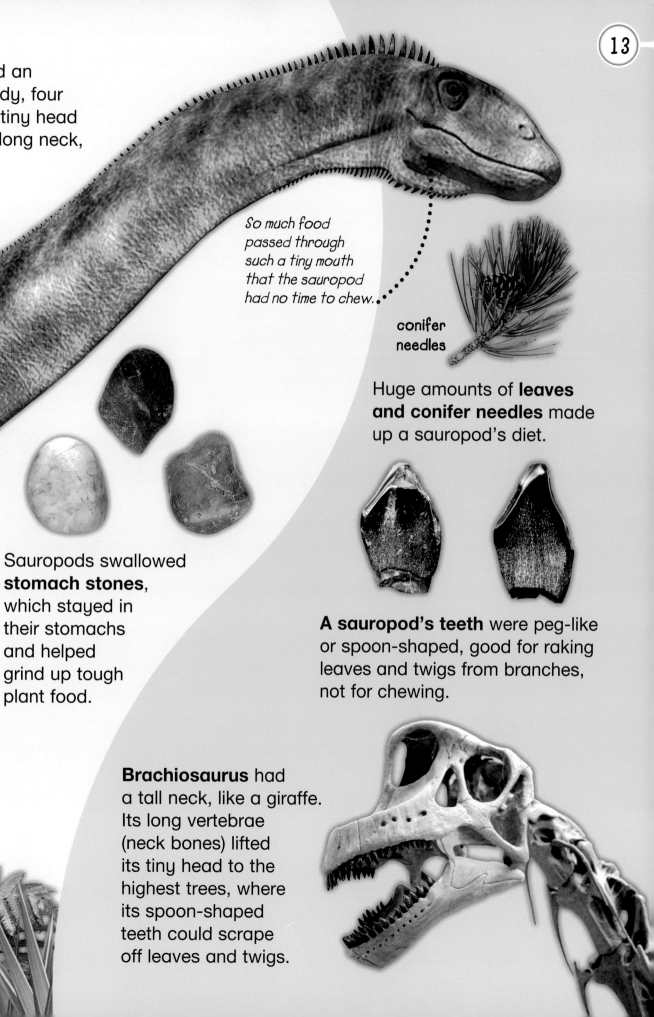

A sauropod had an elephant-like body, four massive legs, a tiny head on the end of a long neck, and a long tail.

Shunosaurus

So much food passed through such a tiny mouth that the sauropod had no time to chew.

conifer needles

Huge amounts of **leaves and conifer needles** made up a sauropod's diet.

Sauropods swallowed **stomach stones**, which stayed in their stomachs and helped grind up tough plant food.

A sauropod's teeth were peg-like or spoon-shaped, good for raking leaves and twigs from branches, not for chewing.

Brachiosaurus had a tall neck, like a giraffe. Its long vertebrae (neck bones) lifted its tiny head to the highest trees, where its spoon-shaped teeth could scrape off leaves and twigs.

A group of Parasaurolophus look up suddenly. Their leader is making a loud trumpeting noise. It may mean danger, or he may be warning them away from other duckbills nearby.

Crested dinosaurs

In the late Cretaceous period, from about 100 million years ago to 65 million years ago, plant-eating dinosaurs called duckbills, or hadrosaurs, were a common sight. Many had strangely shaped crests on top of their heads.

What is this?

Page 23

Page 30

Page 26

This is a jawful of new teeth ready to grow to replace those that get worn down.

Calls and colours

In today's world a lion roars, a cock crows and a peacock shakes its tail – all are ways that these animals use to communicate with one another. It was the same with dinosaurs. The duckbills could communicate both by sound and by visual signals.

Air blew through these hollow bony tubes.

Parasaurolophus had a crest made of hollow bony tubes behind its nostrils. The tubes were used as a kind of trumpet.

A duckbill's jaws were made up of a massive pavement of grinding teeth that were constantly wearing out and then growing back. Duckbills could chew their food thoroughly before swallowing – no stomach stones for them!

Parasaurolophus

Dinosaur colours were probably quite bright, but we don't really know. Duckbills may have had striking patterns so that they could identify one another, or they may have been camouflaged.

Anatotitan could have been this colour...

...or this colour.

The sound made by a Parasaurolophus was probably like a trumpet or trombone.

Sometimes we find fossilized duckbill skin.

Although we know the skin texture, we can only guess the colour.

Tsintaosaurus had a crest that stuck straight up like a unicorn horn.

Olorotitan had a hatchet-shaped crest.

Different duckbills had different crests. Like the horns of antelopes today, the crests helped duckbills to identify the animals that were like them and belonged to their own herds. As well as the different shapes, the crests would have had a range of colours, making each species really distinctive.

Corythosaurus had a semi-circular crest like an ancient Greek helmet.

Dinosaurs with armour

With so many big, fierce meat-eating dinosaurs around, it is no wonder that some of the plant-eaters evolved armour to defend themselves. Horns, plates, neck shields and spikes all appeared on different dinosaurs.

1 Albertosaurus, a fierce predator

2 Edmontonia, protected by back armour

3 tail weapon of blade-like spikes

? This is part of a Styracosaurus skull. The gaps in the neck shield stop it being too heavy.

Page 15

4

5

An Albertosaurus is hunting. It ignores the herds of horned dinosaurs – there are too many of them. Instead it attacks a lone Edmontonia, and is not put off by its armour and spikes.

6

What is this?

?

4 Einiosaurus (left) and Triceratops in the distance

5 Styracosaurus facing danger as a group

6 Styracosaurus with neck shield and horn

Stegosaurus had a double row of plates sticking up along its back. These might have been brightly coloured and used for showing off, but it also had two pairs of spikes at the end of its tail – a serious weapon.

Stegosaurus had armour studs in its neck to protect its throat.

Stegosaurus's plates were probably covered in skin.

heavy tail club made of lumps of bone

Under attack!

Dinosaur life was an arms race! As meat-eaters became bigger and fiercer, the plant-eaters needed more and more elaborate armour in order to defend themselves. Plant-eating dinosaurs had heavy armour made up of different combinations of plates, shields, studs, clubs and vicious horns.

Stegosaurus's tail spikes had a core of bone and an outer coating of horn.

Pachycephalosaurus had a bony dome on its head. This was used not just for fighting enemies. Big males would have fought each other to be leader of the herd.

bony head dome used as a battering ram

thick, bony neck shield

Triceratops was one of several dinosaurs with an armoured shield around the neck. Its three horns all pointed forwards. The animal would turn its armoured head to face approaching danger.

An armoured back and a tail club were Ankylosaurus's defence weapons. The tail was as strong and dangerous as an axe or a medieval club.

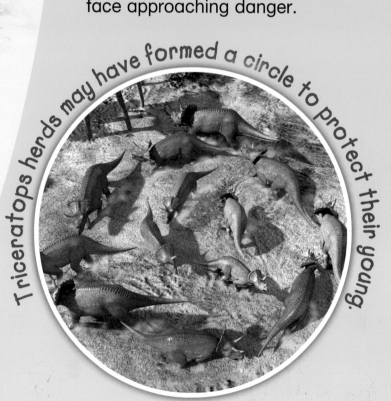

Triceratops herds may have formed a circle to protect their young.

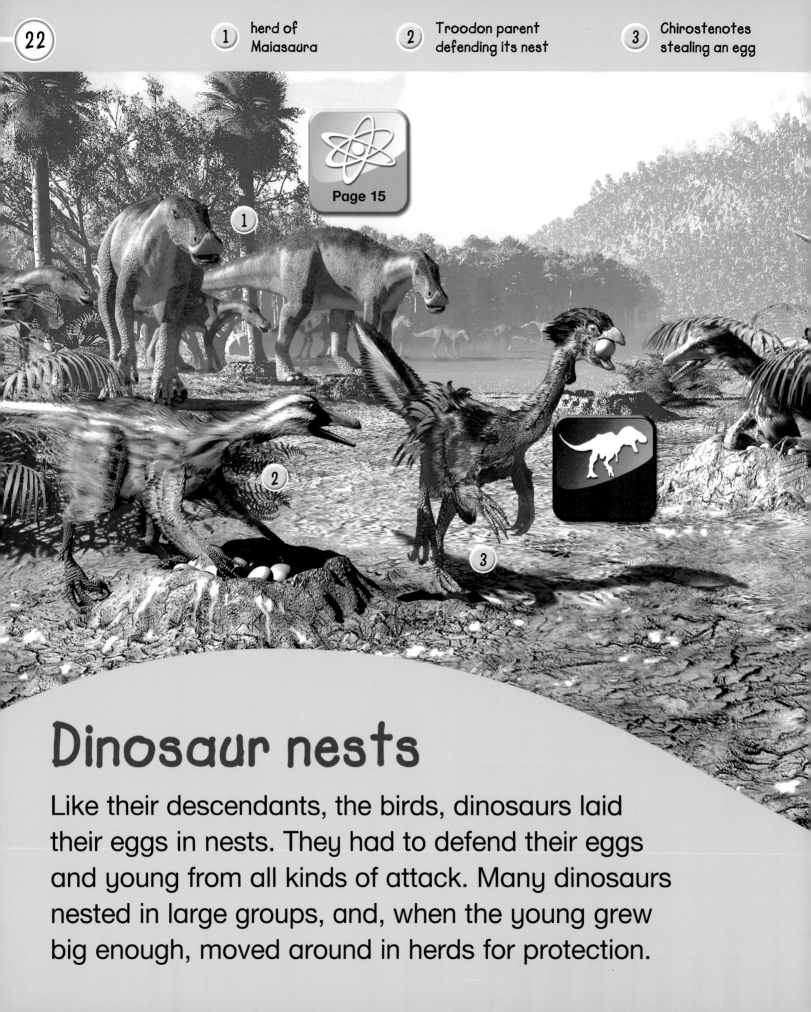

1 herd of
Maiasaura

2 Troodon parent
defending its nest

3 Chirostenotes
stealing an egg

Page 15

Dinosaur nests

Like their descendants, the birds, dinosaurs laid
their eggs in nests. They had to defend their eggs
and young from all kinds of attack. Many dinosaurs
nested in large groups, and, when the young grew
big enough, moved around in herds for protection.

4 Troodon feeding its babies

5 Troodon parent sitting on the nest

6 Troodon baby inside its egg

What is this?

Page 27

4

5

Page 19

Troodon, a small meat-eater, sits on its nest. It is part of a large group, or colony, all nesting together beside a lake during the Cretaceous period. Bigger dinosaurs, like the duckbill Maiasaura, nest in a colony nearby. All the time the dinosaur parents have to guard against egg-stealers such as Chirostenotes.

6

Troodon had feathers very much like these, which belong to a modern eagle.

Growing up

We know quite a lot about dinosaur life. Some lived alone, while others lived in family groups and herds. Fossil eggs and nests tell us about their early lives, and footprints show where they travelled. Sometimes fossils of whole herds are found.

Dinosaur eggs had hard shells, like those of today's birds.

Hatching was a risky time for dinosaurs. Some, like these baby Maiasaura, were looked after by parents. Other dinosaurs could live on their own straight away.

A baby dinosaur had a big head, and big eye sockets.

Eggs and babies are sometimes fossilized, although not usually as perfectly as this. Here a baby Maiasaura has been fossilized while still in the egg.

Fossil trackways show dinosaurs moved in herds.

When on the move, young dinosaurs stayed safely between the enormous adults.

The duckbill Maiasaura built a nest for its eggs and young.

Eggs in the nest were covered by soft vegetation.

Herds of dinosaurs migrated from one feeding ground to another. The parents protected their young from attack.

Page 30

What is this?

① Volcanic gases add to the damage.

② Triceratops, a plant-eater, faces starvation.

③ Quetzalcoatlus, a flying reptile, will die out.

What happened?

Suddenly, 65 million years ago, all the dinosaurs vanished. We think that a giant meteorite struck the Earth and caused so much damage that the dinosaurs could not survive. Around 50 to 80 per cent of all animal and plant life died out too.

3

4

5

Page 30

A meteorite hurtles through the atmosphere. A few seconds later it will hit the Earth and explode, killing everything nearby. Dust and steam thrown up will change the climate for many years. This will kill the plants and cause the death of plant-eating animals and then of meat-eaters.

6

This is a duckbill's beak. It is made of horn with a sharp edge, used for scraping twigs and leaves.

The story so far

Sometimes a dead dinosaur would fall into a river and be buried by sand. Over time the sand would turn to rock and the bones to mineral. Millions of years later, that rock might be worn away by the weather, revealing the fossil. Only then can we find it.

Some flowering plants survived when dinosaurs died out.

Around 65 million years ago, the dinosaurs became extinct (died out), along with three-quarters of all other animal species. Afterwards a new set of animals evolved and repopulated the Earth.

the meteorite impact

Palaeontologists are scientists who study the ancient life of the Earth. Through their work we can find out about the animals and plants of long ago – including dinosaurs.

palaeontologists uncovering a sauropod skeleton

Finding a whole dinosaur skeleton is rare. More often the remains are incomplete, and some dinosaurs are known from only a single bone.

Discovering dinosaurs in a museum is great fun. But a mounted skeleton is the result of years of careful excavation and study.

A dinosaur in a museum is usually made from the parts of different skeletons.

Dinosaur fossils are not made of the original bone – that has been replaced by mineral.

These boxes contain fossilized dinosaur dung.

Dinosaur remains are taken to a laboratory to be studied. Different palaeontologists are experts in different types of fossils. Some study bones, while some study footprints or even dung.

Ceratosaurus on the attack

Some **meat-eaters** hunted alone. Others hunted in packs. Small and medium-sized hunters, such as Ceratosaurus, would have found it easier to hunt big prey in groups.

Chirostenotes

Eggs are a very nutritious (energy-rich) food. Some meat-eating dinosaurs, such as Chirostenotes, probably robbed other dinosaur nests.

Nature

At the start of the age of dinosaurs, Earth's **plants** were mostly ferns and conifers. There was no grass. By the end of the dinosaur age, broadleaved trees had evolved.

Dragonfly

Insects were some of the first land creatures. They evolved 200 million years before the dinosaurs appeared. Today there are several million species of insects.

Dinosaur lives

Many dinosaurs **lived in herds** for protection against meat-eaters. They migrated from one feeding ground to another as the seasons changed.

We know that at least some dinosaurs built **nests**, laid eggs and looked after the youngsters when they hatched – just like birds do today.

a duckbill's nest

Science

long-necked Brachiosaurus

If scientists find a complete dinosaur **skeleton**, they can see straight away what the animal looked like. More often they find just part of a skeleton, or bones scattered about.

Fossilized footprints give us clues about dinosaur life – whether they ran or walked, and how many of them moved about together. It is impossible to tell what dinosaur made what footprint, though.

More to explore

Diplodocus, a sauropod

Sauropods ate plants. They were a bit like vacuum cleaners, standing in one place while their long necks hosed around for food.

Tyrannosaurus, one of the biggest and the last of the meat-eaters, had jaw muscles that were powerful enough to crush all your bones, and a mouth big enough to swallow you whole.

There were many other types of **reptiles** living in the age of dinosaurs. Crocodiles, turtles and the ancestors of all modern lizards, like this one, scuttled around the dinosaurs' feet.

Mammals appeared when the dinosaurs did. Throughout dinosaur times they were small and insignificant. Only when the dinosaurs died out did they become the most important animals on Earth.

Cimolestes

Some dinosaurs had clever ways of **defending** themselves from predators. Styracosaurus probably crowded together so that their horns and shields could protect the whole herd.

Styracosaurus

Dinosaurs could hear well and they could also see well. Some, like the duckbills, could **communicate** to one another using visual displays and loud noises.

meteorite

Sometimes we find fossils of **dinosaur skin**. Then we can see if the animal's surface was scaly or leathery, or even feathered.

Scientists study the **extinction** of the dinosaurs by looking at the rocks of the time – rocks full of meteorite dust, damage from tsunamis and layers of charcoal from forest fires.

Index

In this index, each dinosaur name has a pronunciation guide in brackets.